Learning to Say Goodbye

We dedicate this book to
George Matthews and Stevie Stock,
who reminded us of lessons learned from loss,
how miracles exist in ways we weren't expecting,
and how precious life is.

Goodbyes are only good because we will see our loved ones again.
We honor all those whose hearts' break when they have to say goodbye too soon.

Published by Jo Dee Lang
ISBM #978-1-63901-407-1

LEARNING TO SAY GOODBYE

Written by Cassidy Hitchcock and Jo Dee Lang
Illustrated by McKenzie Green

Learning to say goodbye is never fun.
It means the laughing and playing are done.

Sometimes the saber fights last the whole day.
We sigh, "See you later, wish I could stay!"

At other times, you wave and shout, "Bye bye,"
pedaling home after a grand bike ride.

Adventures end with roasted marshmallows,
sand covered toes, or "Hasta luegos."

Though some goodbyes are not really that bad,
if you'll see them soon, you're not quite as sad.

Share your feelings when farewells last too long.
Others can comfort and help you be strong.

Cause some goodbyes are tougher than others,
and some days may be rougher than others.

With tears we say, "Until we meet again."
We'll see them once more; we're just unsure when.

Hardest of all is, "See you on the other side."
Rely on the Lord, knowing it's okay to cry.

It's heavy knowing it's their time to go.
You may have to search, but each storm has a rainbow.

When there is a day when you're feeling blue,
cuddle their blanket like they snuggled you.

For a loved one is never truly gone.
In the small moments is where they live on.

You'll find yourself watching cartoons like a kid,
laughing and smiling just like they did.

You'll see a dancing bright red balloon
and bounce along humming their favorite tune.

You'll order a donut covered in sprinkles,
just to remember how their eyes twinkled.

Each night when you see the stars in the sky,
Wherever you are they're whispering *hi.*

The simple things can still bring you joy:
fresh painted nails or a soft, favorite toy.

The love and the moments continue on.
We rise up hopeful with each breaking dawn.

Making each moment count with *love you more,*
soon we'll be embracing on the same shore.

Cause learning to say goodbye is never fun,
but a family forever is what we have won.

About the Authors—Cassidy Hitchcock and Jo Dee Lang

We belong to The Church of Jesus Christ of Latter-day Saints and believe in a literal resurrection. Our faith provides hope and peace through good and hard times, but faith doesn't take away grief. In 2016, we said a final earthly goodbye to our 18 month old nephew and grandson. We were heartbroken. We prayed for a miracle that came in other ways besides him being healed. When we heard of our dear friends, whose 3 year old daughter was diagnosed and shortly after passed away from DIPG, wounds were torn open. It didn't seem fair, but somehow we still trusted in God's will. We saw miracles that gave us strength to move forward and rise up more committed to our faith, life, and love. We still recognize the presence of those passed on in small quiet moments. At times tears still come because grief isn't about stages, it's the ebb and flow as the days become our lives. If allowed, grief can be halting; but it can also humble, refine, and strengthen us. We become more than we were because of the love we share. We hope this book brings comfort and reassurance that our loved ones are not gone. There are tender mercies that will come and the best is yet to come.

About the Illustrator—McKenzie Green

Growing up with both of these families I was saddened by the loss of these children. I felt compelled to help in any way possible to the families that have shown my own family so much kindness. I can only hope by sharing my talents I can help in some way to carry some pain and grief. The loss of a loved one is a difficult part of this life. It is my wish that the love and message in this book will provide comfort during the bitter times in life.

CPSIA information can be obtained
at www.ICGtesting.com
Printed in the USA
LVRC091615030921
696875LV00003B/44